Pyramids
of Egypt

Shirley Duke

P9-DGY-486

Before Reading:

Building Academic Vocabulary and Background Knowledge

Before reading a book, it is important to tap into what your child or students already know about the topic. This will help them develop their vocabulary, increase their reading comprehension, and make connections across the curriculum.

1. *Look at the cover of the book. What will this book be about?*
2. *What do you already know about the topic?*
3. *Let's study the Table of Contents. What will you learn about in the book's chapters?*
4. *What would you like to learn about this topic? Do you think you might learn about it from this book? Why or why not?*
5. *Use a reading journal to write about your knowledge of this topic. Record what you already know about the topic and what you hope to learn about the topic.*
6. *Read the book.*
7. *In your reading journal, record what you learned about the topic and your response to the book.*
8. *After reading the book complete the activities below.*

Content Area Vocabulary
Read the list. What do these words mean?

archaeologists
civilization
Egyptologists
flax
hieroglyph
mastabas
papyrus
pharaohs
pyramidiums
quarry
scaffolding
silty
stonemasons
tombs

After Reading:

Comprehension and Extension Activity

After reading the book, work on the following questions with your child or students in order to check their level of reading comprehension and content mastery.

1. *Explain how the pyramids helped give the pharaohs immortality.* (Asking questions)
2. *Why do you think pharaohs wanted to create pyramid-shaped tombs?* (Infer)
3. *Explain the importance of the Nile River in the constructing of the pyramids.* (Summarize)
4. *Why were narrow air shafts built into the pyramids?* (Infer)
5. *What techniques and tools used by the ancient Egyptians are still used today?* (Asking questions)

Extension Activity

Using a computer, look up the Egyptian hieroglyphic alphabet. Using the book, paint or draw a scene that corresponds with what you learned in the text. Write a sentence or two about your scene using the Egyptian hieroglyphics. Give your picture and the symbols with their letters and sound to a teacher, parent, or classmate to translate.

Table of Contents

Monumental Pyramids

Great pyramids line the dry desert on the west side of the Nile River in Egypt. **Pharaohs**, the rulers of ancient Egypt, built these massive stone structures.

Pyramids were first built about 4,500 years ago. They served as **tombs** for Egypt's pharaohs. The pharaohs believed the pyramids would help them have eternal life.

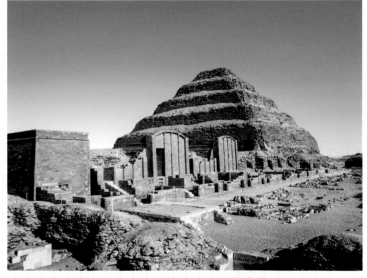

A 30 foot (10 meter) wall surrounded the Step Pyramid and buildings around it in Saqqara. The buildings included temples, chapels, and courtyards.

Through the years, pyramids were built in different ways. They were made of huge slabs of stone and brick. Granite and limestone were cut from a **quarry** and moved down the Nile River.

The bricks were made from river mud, straw, and sand. The workers pressed the mixture into wooden molds. They sat in the heat until they hardened. The pyramid was then covered with other types of stone.

Pyramid stones fitted together closely. Erosion through the years wore down the stones so the blocks now appear to have separations.

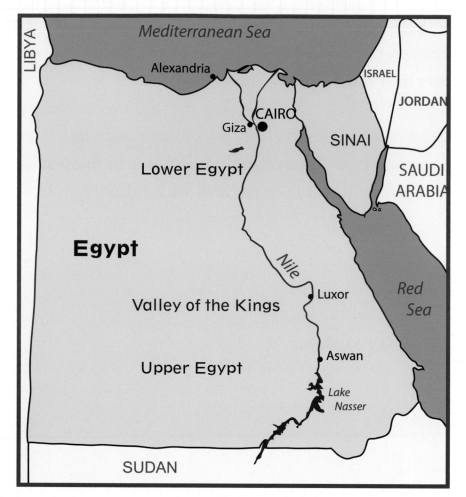

The Nile River is the longest river in the world. It supplied the ancient Egyptians with transportation, food, building materials, and water.

About 80 pyramids still exist in Egypt. The three best-known pyramids are at Giza, near modern-day Cairo. The largest of the three was built for the pharaoh Khufu.

Archaeologists aren't sure why the pharaohs chose the pyramid shape for their monuments. Some think the shape may be a symbol of the sun's rays or a pathway to heaven. The ancient Egyptians believed death was the beginning of a trip to another world. Each person's eternal life depended on the pharaoh. Building the pyramids for their pharaoh would benefit everyone in the kingdom.

The pyramids at Giza were built so the pharaohs could watch from their palaces as they rose. The construction took many years and each pharaoh hoped to live long enough to see his pyramid finished. The cost of these giant tombs was enormous.

The pharaohs gave grand names to the pyramids. Khufu named his Great Pyramid "Khufu is one belonging to the horizon."

Brain Builder!

Khufu's Great Pyramid rose to a height of about 45 stories (481 feet; 147 meters). The base measured 755 feet (230 meters) along each side. It was the tallest structure in the world for more than 4,000 years until the Eiffel Tower was built in Paris, France. The Great Pyramid was one of the seven wonders of the ancient world and the only ancient wonder still standing today.

The mastaba, or tomb, of Seshemnefer IV includes a group of rooms, worship area, and burial chamber. It sits in front of the Great Pyramid at Giza and is the most visited mastaba. Seshemnefer oversaw the two seats of the House of Life and was keeper of the king's secrets.

A pyramid contains a burial chamber for the pharaoh. Some also include a chamber for the queen. A series of tunnels connects other rooms and galleries. Narrow shafts allow air inside.

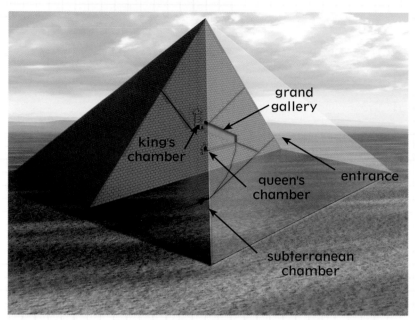

The interior of the Great Pyramid of Giza has three chambers. It is the only Egyptian pyramid known to have both ascending and descending passages.

Brain Builder!

Pharaohs were buried with everything they might need, including food, drinks, pottery, jewelry, furniture, and other treasures. A boat was often buried next to the pyramid for the pharaoh to use in the afterlife.

The Egyptians also preserved the pharaoh's intestines, stomach, lungs, and liver for the afterlife. They did not save the brain, because they believed it was worthless.

Canopic jars were used to store and preserve the internal organs. Each jar featured the head of an Egyptian god.

Tales of treasures buried with the pharaohs tempted tomb robbers. To keep thieves out of the tombs, huge stones weighing up to three tons were set in the passages and at the entrances.

The pyramid builders also carved false doors into the bases. Some tunnels were disguised or had blind passages and trapdoors with locks. Still, only one pharaoh's burial site wasn't robbed: that of Tutankhamun, who was buried in an underground tomb in the Valley of the Kings. He was found lying in a series of three coffins, the final one gold. Bracelets, rings, collars, and thousands of other priceless objects were found with him.

The tomb of King Tutankhamun contained artworks and other ritual objects ancient Egyptians believed would provide for the pharaoh's afterlife.

Ancient Egypt

Ancient Egypt was 95 percent desert. The region also held the Nile River. Fertile, **silty** soil left by regular flooding lined its banks. The Nile was a source of life for the people living near it. It also served as the main route for transportation.

A well-developed **civilization** rose in the Old Kingdom of Egypt about 5,000 years ago. The word pharaoh meant great house. Later the title came to mean king. People believed the pharaohs were gods and their eternal lives depended on the king's life.

A pharaoh led the army, controlled the treasury, and acted as a judge. Egypt was divided in two parts—Upper and Lower Egypt. The pharaoh kept the two regions together.

Because pharaohs controlled the money, they had resources to build their pyramids. They hired the finest engineers, **stonemasons**, and workers to build their monuments.

Brain Builder!

Pharaohs held the highest social rank. Nobles, officials, soldiers, and scribes ranked below the ruling pharaoh. Skilled workers and merchants were ranked next. Most of the people were peasant farmers and servants.

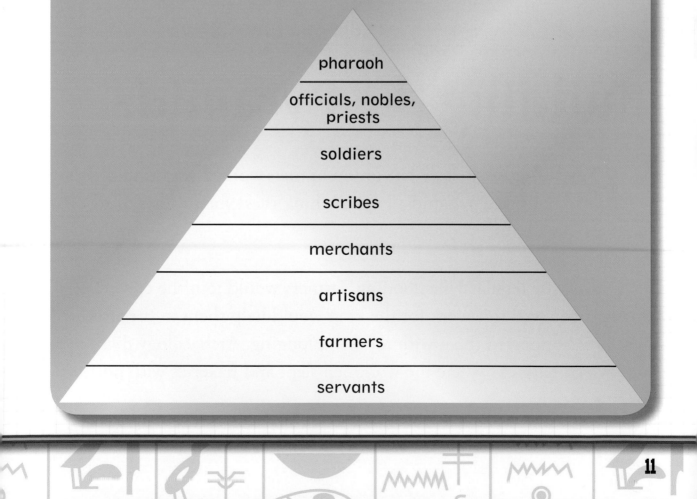

pharaoh

officials, nobles, priests

soldiers

scribes

merchants

artisans

farmers

servants

Dr. Selim Bey Hassan of the University of Cairo was a renowned archaeologist. In this late 1930s photo, he exhibits pottery from an excavation.

Dr. Selim Bey Hassan (1886-1961)

Building the Pyramids

Egyptologists believe one group of men worked year-round to build the pyramids. Experts think these men were skilled workers, not slaves.

During the regular Nile flooding, farmers would join the crew. The workers believed this work for the king would help them in the afterlife. The king supported them with food and lodging. Archaeology digs have uncovered barracks where the workmen slept and bakeries with pots for baking bread.

Evidence from archaeologists shows organization in the gangs of workers. One gang was divided into two crews. Each crew was divided into five phyles, a Greek word meaning tribe.

Each phyle held divisions that were identified by a symbolic name, written as a **hieroglyph**, a type of Egyptian picture writing. The work gangs wrote graffiti on the stones using their symbols to identify their group and the king's name.

This pillar relief from the Meinet Habu temple at Luxor shows the goddess Hathor and pharaoh Rameses. A relief is a sculpture that appears to be raised by carving away parts of the stone.

Brain Builder!

Before written language, ancient Egyptians used pictures called hieroglyphs. These included symbols for numbers up to one million. Much is known about ancient Egypt because of these picture records, kept mostly by priests. They can be read from both directions. The figures faced toward the start of the line. The pictures could stand for a sound or an entire word. Scribes used a shortened version of hieroglyphics called hieratic when they needed to write quickly. François Champollion, a Frenchman, cracked the code for reading hieroglyphics in 1822 from ancient writings inscribed on the Rosetta Stone, which was discovered in 1799.

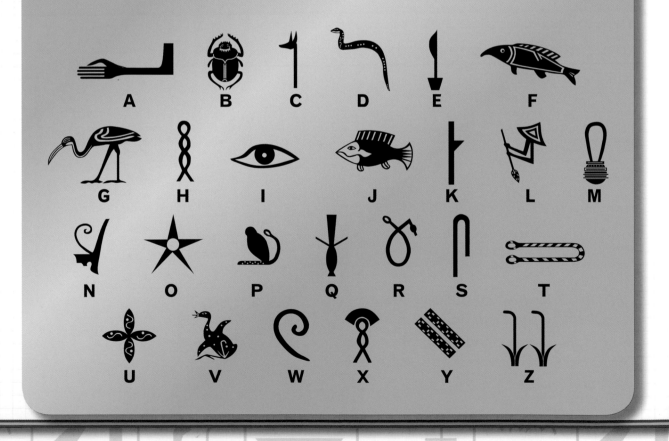

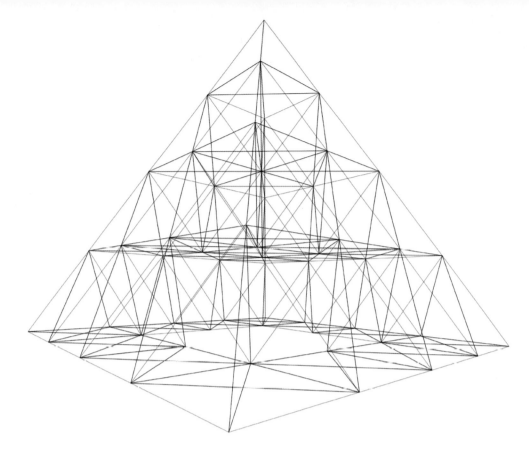

The pharaoh's master builder, the vizier, oversaw the building of a pyramid using plans developed by engineers. Their techniques are still an engineering wonder today. A vizier was the highest official to serve a pharaoh.

Engineering the Pyramids

Pyramid building is based on civil engineering. The Egyptians used an advanced method of design and building for that time period. Some practices they developed are still used today.

In Ancient Egypt, architects designed the pyramids and other buildings. Engineers carried out the designs and made adjustments as construction progressed on a project.

The Step Pyramid was the first large stone monument. King Djoser ordered it built in 2680 BCE. Imhotep, an architect, first applied large-scale technology to its construction.

Built about 4,700 years ago, the Step Pyramid of Djoser featured six layers built in stages with underground tunnels below.

The design included **mastabas**, flat-roofed buildings with sloping sides stacked on top of the other. The six mastabas grew smaller on each of the upper layers. The final pyramid looked like a set of giant steps. Workers covered the outer layer of stone with polished limestone.

Brain Builder!

Imhotep, the first known architect, lived between 2667 BCE - 2648 BCE and is known as the founder of Egyptian architecture and astronomy. His job title was Director of Works for Upper and Lower Egypt. Imhotep was also a scribe, writer, priest, and doctor. As one of Pharaoh Djoser's advisors, he designed the Step Pyramid at Sakkara. He became the patron saint of scribes and was known as a local god due to his medical cures and advice. Imhotep grew even more famous than his ruler in later years.

Pyramids were built on the west side of the Nile, where the Sun set. The construction site needed to be close to the river for stone delivery.

The four sides of a pyramid's base had to line up with true north, south, east, and west. This made right angles at the four corners. Because the magnetic compass had not been invented, engineers used other methods to find directions. They used the North Star to find north. They used the equinoxes or shadows cast by the Sun to locate east and west.

Giza Necropolis, also called the Giza pyramid complex, is located on the Giza Plateau near Cairo, Egypt. The complex includes Khufu's Great Pyramid.

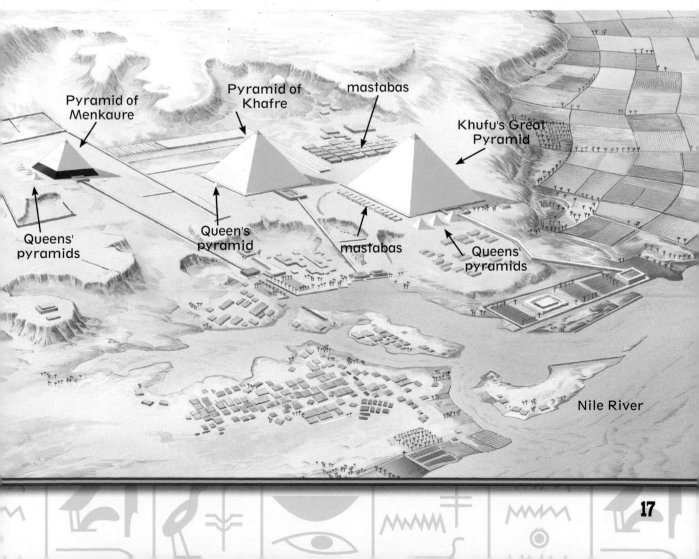

The base of a pyramid had to support the enormous weight of the finished structure. Pyramids were built on rock, gravel, or sand. They had to be leveled, but rock bases made that more difficult.

Uneven surfaces were built up or slabs of stone were added to make the pyramid level. Uneven bases used a comparison line to level the pyramid. At times, bricks were used to mark the lines where it would be built. A few of these bricks can be seen today on some pyramids.

This pyramid's walls were built of yellow limestone bricks.

Most of the stones used for the pyramids were quarried from the Giza Plateau. White limestone covering the outside were from Tura. Granite stones came from Aswan. Edges were so well cut the seams lined up perfectly.

The stone slabs could weigh up to two and a half tons. More than 2,300,000 blocks had to pushed or dragged into place on Khufu's Great Pyramid. The cuts of the stone surfaces were made so accurately that they changed only about one hundredth of an inch. The stones fit together so closely a knife couldn't fit between them.

Engineers designed the complex series of burial chambers, passages, and other rooms inside the pyramids. The passages were built so well that the angles and width never changed more than a half inch.

Cornerstones were built in with balls and sockets, much like current bridge designs. These joints let the pyramids expand and contract in changing temperatures. The joints allowed the stones to withstand earthquakes and sandstorms.

This amazing engineering all took place at a time around the end of the pre-history period. These remarkable achievements demonstrate the abilities of early engineers.

Brain Builder!

Experts think the Egyptians built the Giza Pyramids over a period of 85 years, between 2589 and 2504 BCE.

The doors of pyramids were built above the ground and sealed with a huge stone to deter tomb robbers. Stairs were added centuries later to allow easier access in and out for the Egyptologists.

Brain Builder!

Herodotus, a Greek historian known as the father of history, was the first to write about the pyramids after visiting them in 440 BCE, about 2,000 years after they were built. He described the polished limestone casing over the stone slabs. He also wrote that he could hardly see the joints between the stones.

Herodotus
(circa 484–425 BCE)

Engineers and architects wrote the plan designs and figures on **papyrus** for some of the later pyramids. Mathematical equations helped them determine the correct angles and dimensions.

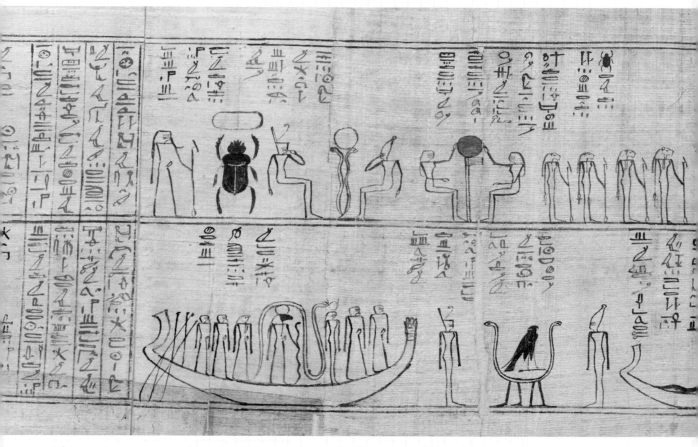

This ancient papyrus features Egyptian hieroglyphics, one of the oldest writing systems in the world.

The angle of the sides was equal to half the width of the base, divided by its height, and then multiplied by seven. Scribes wrote down everything, including the number of stones used, tool lists, and the excuses ill workers gave for missing work.

Pyramid foundations, often built on a plateau area, were marked using a tool called a level pegging. The tool had a wooden peg and a cord made from **flax**.

The workers dug trenches and filled them with water to mark the level. Then they removed all the unleveled surfaces until it was flat. The Egyptians were so accurate that one corner of the Great Pyramid is only a half inch (1.3 centimeters) higher than the opposite corner.

Flax plants provided fibers for making rope and cords. Today it is also used for fine lace and linen. The plant stems are soaked until the outside covering comes off, leaving soft, flexible fibers that can be made into cord and rope or spun for cloth.

Priests blessed the foundation because the base of the structures were believed to have magical properties. This is much like today's practice of inviting a well-known person to attend ground-breaking ceremonies or place the first stone on new buildings.

Local limestone was the main building material. Stonemasons cut this somewhat soft stone from quarries near Giza.

High-quality limestone from Tura, across the river, formed the outer casing. The kind of stone used also depended on the pyramid's location. Quarries nearest the site determined what stone was used. Other types of stone were imported from faraway places.

Bas-relief like this decorated the inside of the chapel of Anubis, part of the Temple of Hatshepsut. Bas-relief is a type of sculpture in which shapes are carved so they are only a little higher than the flat background. Even with part of the monument in ruins, the Temple of Hatshepsut is considered by many to be the most beautiful of all the ancient Egyptian temples.

Some bas-reliefs found during excavations are on display at the Louvre Museum in Paris, France.

Cornerstones, casing stone, and granite had to be ordered by the master builder and cut to certain dimensions. Each stone was marked and sent to the building site, where the master builder inspected each one.

Brain Builder!

Broken pieces of limestone and sandstone sometimes served as writing material because papyrus was so expensive.

After cutting to exact measurements, stones were transported to barges and moved down the Nile to the building site.

Each stone had to fit accurately when set into position. The stones were cut to the correct dimensions at the quarry. A stone with the wrong dimensions was cut to the right size in a workshop at the pyramid's base.

Builders often used granite to line the inside chambers and passages. This hard stone was shipped along the Nile from quarries near Aswan, about 500 miles (805 kilometers) up the river. Mined copper and other metals for tools came from the Sinai area.

To form a pyramid, four sides had to angle upward and meet at the top to make a point. Pyramids were built layer by layer from the bottom. The builders checked their measurements often. A small mistake at the bottom would be a big problem at the top if not corrected.

The quarried stone moved downriver on barges with sails. Barge travel on the river was the only available transportation.

When the Nile flooded each year, a natural harbor formed. It is thought the harbor may have remained open all year.

Moving the stones to the barge and construction sites required the use of simple machines such as levers, pulleys, and ramps.

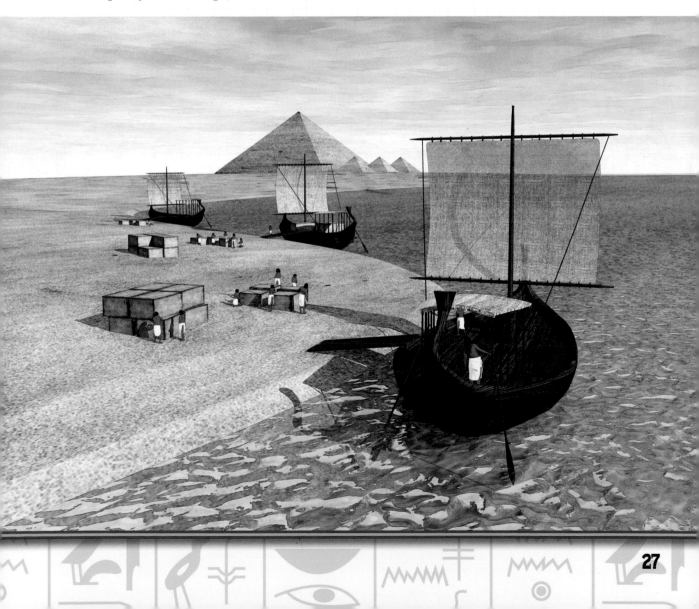

Workers unloaded the stones as close to the construction site as possible. Extra heavy loads were put on sleds with runners and pulled by a team of men.

To reduce friction, workers wet the sand so the drag wouldn't pile up the sand in front of the sledge.

Brain Builder!

Safety was a problem in pyramid building. The large stone slabs were cut from a quarry. They were moved down the river by barges. Nile flooding made transporting the huge slabs difficult at times. The barges could drift away or run aground.

Flash floods took place at times. At one point, the ancient Egyptians built a dam across part of the desert to keep the loads safe from flash floods.

Construction accidents also occurred. Evidence from archaeological digs shows skeletons with hand bones supported by wood on both sides as well as evidence of other injuries.

Workers set the stones into place once they were delivered. As the pyramid grew higher, the stones had to be lifted higher. The workers built ramps alongside the work area and raised them with the growing pyramid.

Teams of men pulled the heavy stones. A main ramp may have led to the upper work area, with lanes for going up and down.

Work continued until the structure was complete. **Scaffolding** supported the workers as the pyramid grew higher. Then the ramps and scaffolding were taken down.

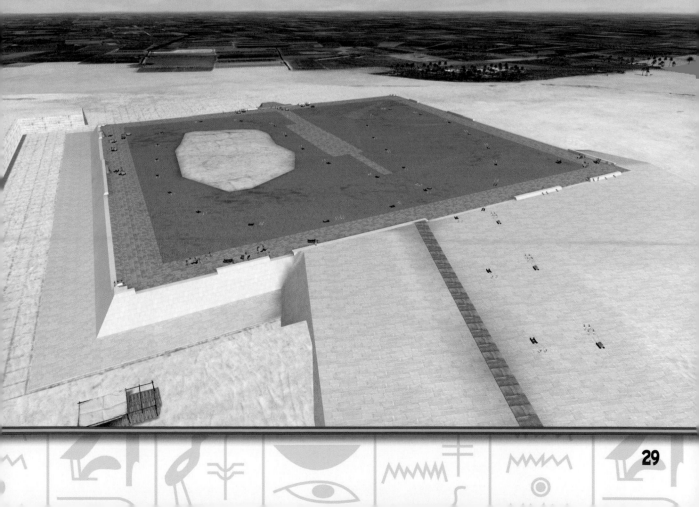

Ramps gave workers access to the pyramid as it grew. The outer casing was immediately added after the building stones were put into place so the pyramid rose as a finished structure.

Copper tools proved too soft for stonework. Masons used a pounder made of granite or dolorite, a hard type of rock. The Egyptians also had axes, and carpenters used adzes, a tool for chopping and planing wood.

Excavators have found models of other tools from a later date than when the Great Pyramids were built. A pull saw blade and a model knife-like saw were used for cutting wood. Wooden clamps held stones together. Masons' hammers of hard wood beat on chisels made of copper or bronze for detailed work. Builders rubbed the rock slabs with smooth stones for a final polishing after they were set in place.

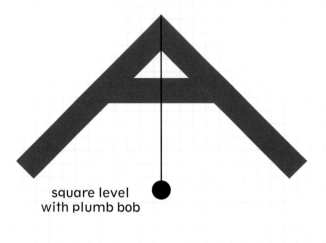

square level
with plumb bob

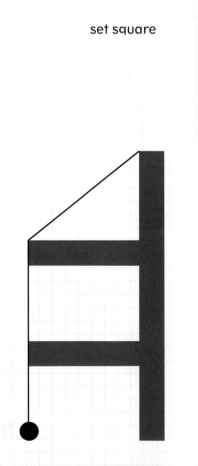

set square

verticle plumb bob

Brain Builder!

Ancient Egyptians used special tools to get precise measurements while constructing the pyramids. The set square measured right angles. The plumb bob was used to attain accurate vertical angles. The square level, an A-shaped wooden frame with legs of equal length, measured horizontal surfaces.

Brain Builder!

When Waynman Dixon discovered the unfinished ventilation shafts leading off the Queen's Tomb in the Great Pyramid, he found two ancient tools left there. They were a granite pounding stone and a metal hook. A third tool, a foot-long (.3 meter) piece of cedar wood with notches cut into it, disappeared. It's not known what happened to it. Archaeologists think workmen may have left them there. No other tools exist from the Giza pyramids. These tools remained in the Dixon family until they donated them to the British Museum in the 1970s.

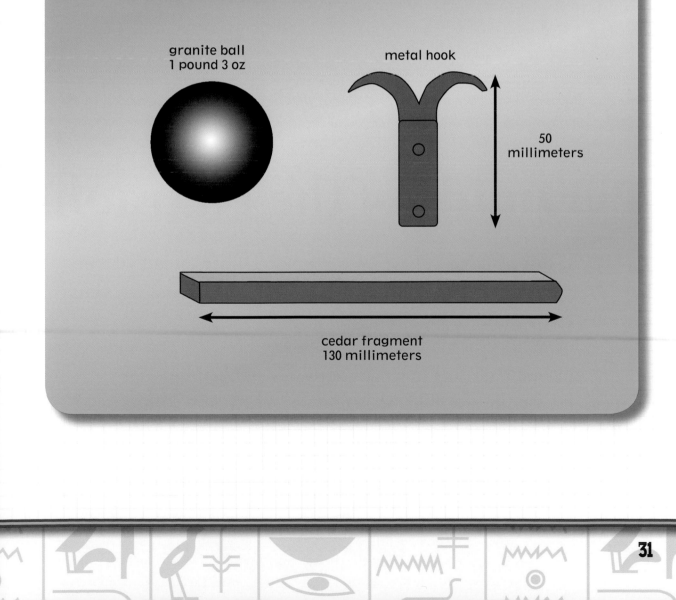

granite ball
1 pound 3 oz

metal hook

50 millimeters

cedar fragment
130 millimeters

The Step Pyramid holds different rooms and tunnels that were built into the structure, much like the later pyramids. It includes a burial chamber for the pharaoh, King Djoser.

Pyramids of the Pharaohs

The first pyramid in Egypt was Pharaoh Djoser's Step Pyramid. It was built at Sakkara about 2680 BCE. Djoser and five family members were buried there.

The pharaoh built a set of stone courtyards and buildings for ceremonies near the pyramid. The entry was sealed with a three-ton (3.05 metric ton) plug. Later pharaohs also built step pyramids.

Sneferu was the first pharaoh to build the well-known smooth pyramid shape, sometime around 2600 BCE. Building methods had improved by this time. The workers built the pyramid with larger stone blocks. Architects used a new roofing method above the burial chamber. The design supported the heavy stones better. They also improved ways of sealing off the entry.

The pyramid seemed to be designed with steep sides, however, this made it somewhat unstable. The builders changed the angle a little, giving it a slightly bent look. It is called the Bent Pyramid.

This bent pyramid is the best-preserved example.

Khufu, Sneferu's son, had the Great Pyramid built for him at Giza. It was the largest of all the pyramids.

Great Pyramid Facts

Height: 480.69 feet (147 meters)
40 stories high (433 feet; 132 meters)

Length:
West side 755.76 feet (230.3 meters)
North side 755.41 feet (230.2 meters)
East side 755.87 feet (230.4 meters)
South side 756.08 feet (230.5 meters)

Area of the Base: 13 acres (5.3 hectares)
Number of Blocks: more than 2.5 million
Weight of Blocks: 2-70 tons each
(1.8 metric tons-64 metric tons)
Size of original limestone casing stones:
Some weighed 15 tons each (14 metric tons)

Ascending Passage:
Height 3.94 feet (1.2 meters)
Length 97.6 feet (29.7 meters)
Width 3.4 feet (1.04 meters)
Slope 26 degrees

Descending Passage:
Height 3.94 feet (1.2 meters)
Length 344.3 feet (105 meters)
Width 3.4 feet (1.04 meters)
Slope 26 degrees 30 minutes

King's Chamber:
Length 34.38 feet (10.5 meters)
Width 17.19 feet (5.2 meters)
Height (to floor surface) 17.1 feet
(5.2 meters)
Height (to true base) 19.2 feet (5.9 meters)

Khafra's pyramid was shorter than the Great Pyramid built by his father, Khufu. It appears taller because the base was placed on higher ground. He, too, surrounded his pyramid with a bigger, more complex courtyard.

Khafra's tomb area featured many statues, including the Sphinx. The workmen carved the Sphinx from the bedrock in front of the pyramid.

The Sphinx represents the pharaoh in the form of a lion with a human head. It is wearing the typical headdress of a pharaoh.

Khafra's son Menkaure called for construction of a smaller pyramid, a tenth of the size of his father's. He used expensive granite to cover the bottom levels and included a granite burial chamber.

When Menkaure died suddenly, his heir likely completed the building but used mud brick. South of his pyramid, Menkaure built three smaller pyramids for his wives and possibly daughters, although they were never finished either.

Brain Builder!

A burial coffin, or sarcophagus, was found in Menkaure's burial chamber in the 1800s. It was shipped to England, but the ship sank in the Mediterranean and the coffin went down with it.

The Pyramid of Menkaure and Pyramids of Queens. The Pyramid of Khafre and Pyramid of Khufu, the Great Pyramid, can be seen in the background.

Pyramid of Khafre

Pyramid of Menkaure

Khufu's Great Pyramid

Queens' pyramids

The memorial burial temple of Mentuhotep II incorporated many elements of the pyramids.

After a period of war and disorder, the Middle Kingdom pharaohs again built pyramids.

A block from the sanctuary in the Temple of Mentuhotep II at Deir el-Bahri.

Mentuhotep II became the first pharaoh of the Middle Kingdom. He united Upper and Lower Egypt again. His long, peaceful reign brought back culture and the arts to Egypt. He built his temple against the steep cliffs of Thebes, the capital city. The temple featured painted images and hieroglyphics and an additional building complex.

The next ruling family began with Amenemhat. He built the first true pyramid during the Middle Kingdom. He had it placed there after moving the capital to Lisht. Artists created a series of royal statues that reflected changes in the concept of monarchy.

Senusret III organized the government and conquered Nubia to the south. He built his pyramid at Dahshur. The Step Pyramid influenced his design. The next pharaoh, Amenemhat III, built his black pyramid at Dahshur as well. His complex included two pyramids. He also built a maze and irrigation system with dikes to control the Nile River.

The Black Pyramid was built by King Amenemhat III during Egypt's Middle Kingdom period. It was called the Black Pyramid because of the color of mud used in the inner core that was uncovered as the pyramid crumbled.

By the New Kingdom period, pharaohs were building more temples and tombs instead of pyramids. The last pyramid was built between the Middle Kingdom and the start of the New Kingdom. However, nobles and scribes built **pyramidiums**. They put their own decorated, small tombs in a courtyard.

Brain Builder!

Pyramid professor W. M. Flinders Petrie, an English engineer and archaeologist, made the first exact measurements of the Great Pyramid using steel tapes and special chains. He published them in 1883 in his book, The Pyramids and Temple of Gizeh.

W. M. Flinders Petrie (1853 – 1942)

Statue of Ramesses II in Karnak temple, Luxor, Egypt.

The pyramids of Egypt were built to provide the pharaohs and their people with a way to the afterlife. Thousands worked to quarry rock and construct them.

Experts believe about 20,000 to 25,000 people worked over 20 years to construct the Great Pyramid. This included the people setting stones in place, as well as carpenters, metal workers, and stonecutters. Others worked to provide support, such as potters to make pots for food, water haulers, bakers, and brewers.

Excavation has revealed much about the ancient Egyptian way of life. The evidence found by experts demonstrates a well-developed culture many thousands of years ago.

Archaeologists excavate a site in Thebes, West Bank of Luxor, Egypt.

Tourists visit the ancient Egyptian pyramids. The Giza burial sites have been a popular tourist destination since they were built.

The Pyramids Today

Ancient pharaohs wanted to ensure their immortality. The long-lasting pyramids have endured, allowing the legacy of the pharaohs to live on in modern times.

The pyramids provide an economic boost to Egypt through tourism. Thousands travel to Egypt to visit the remains of this civilization. However, the large number of visitors has been harmful to the ancient and often fragile temples, art, and pyramids. This has happened in different ways.

The pyramids shone white in the sunlight with the outer casing in place. The casing stones have disappeared from the great pyramids. Only the casing at the top of Khafre remains. Both erosion and human activity played a part. People stripped off the pyramids' valuable limestone. They used it for making buildings in Cairo by the 12th century.

Early grave robbers destroyed the buildings and removed valuable artifacts from the tombs. The large number of visitors to the pyramids changes the humidity in the temples, which damages the paintings. Pollution from the cities and demand for water and sewage control speed up the erosion and damage to the structures.

The Pyramid of Khafre, also called the Pyramid of Chephren, is the tomb of the Fourth-Dynasty pharaoh Khafre.

But something is being done. Restoration to the pyramids and temples and changes to improve tourism have begun. Egypt's national treasures provide great resources to the region's history and culture. Preserving and protecting them benefits everyone, allowing present and future generations to experience these great wonders.

Restoration efforts aim to save the Great Step Pyramid of Djoser.

Brain Builder!

Ancient Egyptians buried their dead in the desert, where the heat and dry sand preserved the bodies. Later, the dead were put into coffins to protect them from animals. The bodies decayed in the coffins, so over centuries, the Egyptians developed mummification methods to embalm the bodies and wrapped them in linen strips to preserve them.

This golden shrine was found in Tutankhamun's tomb. Inside was a canopic chest, which contained his internal organs.

Brain Builder!

Pyramids are also found in other countries. In Mexico and Central America, pyramids with steps leading to the tops were built in ancient times. In Teotihuacan, Mexico, the Pyramid of the Sun was built in about 150 CE for the gods. In Guatemala, the Temple of the Giant Jaguar served as a tomb. The Mayans used them for cultural practices. The Aztecs used them for human sacrifice.

Ziggurats, a structure similar to the Egyptian pyramids, has four sides and rises high. The sides are tiered to allow for work on it and for religious rituals. One of the largest is in Ur, Iran.

Rome has a pyramid inspired by the Nubian style. It is believed to date from 15 BCE and was built as a tomb for a magistrate.

Engineering Timeline

2600 BCE *Old Kingdom 2700 BCE - 2200 BCE*

- ▢ Step Pyramid built in layers for the pharaoh Djoser
- ▢ Bent Pyramid built with top half featuring a different slope than the lower half
- ▢ North Pyramid, featuring the first true pyramid shape, built for the pharaoh Senefru

2500 BCE

Pyramids of Giza built:

- ▢ Largest for pharaoh Khufu (also called Cheops)
- ▢ Second largest pyramid built for Khafre, Khufu's son (also called Chephren)
- ▢ Sphinx built to guard Khafre's pyramid
- ▢ Third largest pyramid built for pharaoh Menkaure (also called Mycernius)

2375 BCE

- ▢ Pyramid built for pharaoh Unas is one of first to be decorated inside

2300 BCE *Middle Kingdom 2050 BCE - 1350 BCE*

- ▢ Pyramid construction stops due to period of political instability

2050 BCE

- ▢ Pharaohs resume construction of pyramids

1800 BCE

- ▢ Last of the pyramids are built

1550 – 1086 BCE *New Kingdom 1550 BCE - 1086 BCE*

- ▢ New Kingdom period; pharaohs buried in tombs of cut-out rock

Glossary

archaeologists (ahr-kee-AH-lah-jists): scientists who study the distant past, which often involves removing soil to uncover historical items

civilization (siv-UH-li-ZAY-shuhn): a developed society with organization and culture

Egyptologists (ee-jip-TAHL--jists): people who study the history and language of ancient Egypt

flax (flacks): a plant fiber that can be woven

hieroglyph (hire-uh-GLIF): an ancient way of writing using pictures and symbols

mastabas (mas-TAH-bahs): flat-roofed buildings

papyrus (puh-PYE-rus): a kind of paper made from the stem of a water plant

pharaohs (PHAR-ohs): Egyptian kings or rulers

pyramidiums (pir-uh-MID-ee-ums): decorated, small tombs in the shape of a pyramid

quarry (KWOR-ee): a place where stone is dug out

scaffolding (SKAF-uhld-ing): a temporary platform for workmen

silty (SILT-ee): tiny particles of soil and rock carried in rivers

stonemasons (STONE-may-suhns): workers who cut and shape stone

tombs (TOOMS): graves or buildings built to hold bodies after death

Index

Show What You Know

1. Explain why the pharaohs wanted to build such lasting monuments for themselves.
2. What can you conclude about the Egyptian culture during the time pyramids were being constructed?
3. How did engineers and architects contribute to the pyramids?
4. Why did the people of Egypt believe that helping to construct the pyramids was a good idea?
5. What threatened the pyramids in ancient times? What threatens them now?

Websites to Visit

www.pbs.org/wgbh/nova/ancient/explore-ancient-egypt.html

www.mnh.si.edu/exhibits/eternal-life/

www.pbs.org/wgbh/nova/pyramid/textindex.html

About the Author

Shirley Duke enjoys reading about ancient Egypt and the pyramids. The history of Egyptian engineering is her favorite topic and she likes learning how the Egyptians wrote. Here's her name in hieroglyphics:

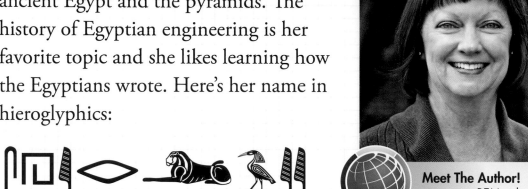

Meet The Author!
www.meetREMauthors.com

www.rourkeeducationalmedia.com

PHOTO CREDITS: Cover © Gurgen Backhshetsyan; title page © HypnoCreative; page 4 © windowseat, meinzahn; page 5 © AndreySt; page 6 © pavalena; page 7 © Mik122; page 8 © Clause Lunau/Science Source, eldeiv/shutterstock; page 9 © Everett Historical; page 10 © grauzikas; page 12 © Library of Congress; page 13 © oversnap; page 14 © Zmrlzna; page 15 © ArtyFree; page 16 © Daniel Fleck/arenadesign.de; page 17 © Gary Hincks/Science Source; page 18 © svetlana Privezentseva; page 19 © Maveric149; page 20 © Steve Heap; page 21 © Marie-Lan Nguyen; page 22 © Javi Martin; page 23 © Anna Yu; page 24, 25, 29 © Jean-Pierre Houdin; page 24 © ewg3D; page 26 © Henning Dalhoff/ Science Photo Library; page 30, 31 © Renee Brady; page 32 Joe Ignacio Soto; page 33 © Gurgen Bakhshetsyan; page 34 © efesenko; page 35 © Pius Lee; page 36 © Kasto; page 37 © Olaf Tausch; page 38 © Tekisch; page 39 © moonfish7; page 40 © berliner; page 41 © oksmit; page 42 © Anton_Ivanov; page 43 © Jose Ignacio Soto, Alan Diaz/AP; page 44 © Tono Balaguer

Edited by: Keli Sipperley

Cover and interior design by: Renee Brady

Library of Congress PCN Data

Pyramids of Egypt / Shirley Duke
(Engineering Wonders)
ISBN 978-1-63430-415-3 (hard cover)
ISBN 978-1-63430-515-0 (soft cover)
ISBN 978-1-63430-606-5 (e-Book)
Library of Congress Control Number: 2015931727

Also Available as:

Printed in the United States of America, North Mankato, Minnesota